RIVER FRIEND

A series of Riverine Small Books

by Sylvia M. Haslam and Tina Bone

BOOK 8

VEGETATION CHANGES OVER TIME

Is there freeze frame?

Eighth published book in the Series:

VEGETATION CHANGES OVER TIME
Is there freeze frame?

A Book in a series of Riverine publications by

Sylvia M. Haslam and Tina Bone

(Each book is about a different subject so the series can be read in any order)

Written and Edited by Sylvia Haslam and Tina Bone. Illustrated by Tina Bone (unless otherwise stated)

RFS8: PAPERBACK **52** pp.
ISBN No. 978 1 9162096 6 4
80 Illustrations

Published by: Tina Bone UK
First edition: **March 2023**

https://riverfriend.tinasfineart.uk
Email: ourbooks@tinasfineart.uk

CONTENTS

INTRODUCTION TO THE SERIES

Rivers are vital. They bring freshwater to the land, on which all its life depends. They are beautiful and fascinating, making up both the typical British countryside and many of its most spectacular views. If they vanished, what hardship and outrage there would be! Yet, slowly, slowly, they are vanishing, the larger stream becomes smaller, the tiny brook becomes a ditch and dries, and is filled in—the small ditches get polluted and dug out, become dull, and vanish from sight and consciousness. How can we save our rivers and riverscapes? How can we raise awareness on this slow, almost invisible loss?

We believe that this series of handy, small books, suitable for readers from teenage upwards, will help to raise awareness. Individually, each book tells a story on a particular riverine and riparian environment. Collectively, the series will inform, in a simple and effective manner, the extraordinary value of freshwater and its plants.

The Authors realised that there was a huge gap in the literature. There are many publications for scientists, for pond-dippers, birders and anglers, but handy pocket books focussing on the river itself, and the vegetation belonging to it and creating the habitat for all else: we could find none!

For explanations regarding British freshwater plants, terminology mentioned throughout the series, and Picture Guide and reference section for further reading, see the book entitled *A PROLOGUE TO THE SERIES: Plant identification and Glossary of Terms* (also available to view in pdf format free on-line at https://riverfriend.tinasfineart.uk/resources/)

Other titles in the Series are listed on the last page of this book and on the River Friend **Website: https://riverfriend.tinasfineart.uk**

VEGETATION CHANGES OVER TIME
Is there freeze frame?

INTRODUCTION

River vegetation varies a lot, is extraordinarily sensitive to its immediate environment and reflects all the habitat factors acting upon it, beginning with those set by geology, history, climate, rock type, landscape, and the part of the river being studied (its size and its landscape). Water makes the river what and where it is. All life needs water. People often talk about the earth's life being carbon-based (mostly). True, but even more it is water-based! Most life forms are composed of at least 80% water. Aquatic plants and animals in addition live part or all of their lives within, on, or by the water.

Take an ordinary water lily for instance: its lily pads and flowers float beautifully on the water, but are touching on, and under, the water on their lower sides. Many species of fish, such as trout and perch, live entirely within the water. So do aquatic plants such as Hornworts (*Ceratophyllum demersum*, Rigid hornwort, Fig. 1a, and *Ceratophyllum submersum*, Soft hornwort, Fig. 1b),

Fig. 1c. Difference between the two plants.

Ceratophyllum demersum: *two points and stiff*

Ceratophyllum submersum: *soft, lots of points and floppy*

Fig. 1a Rigid Hornwort (Ceratophyllum demersum)

Fig. 1b Soft hornwort (Ceratophyllum submersum)

and Shoreweed (*Littorella uniflora*, Fig. 2).

*Fig. 2. Shoreweed (*Littorella uniflora*)—small plant which grows in slow-moving rivers or lakes. Leaves are 2–10cm long*

This book is about change, and what changes may take place, and when, and why. To freeze-frame when filming moving objects is to hold a still picture at one instant in time. The same applies with the [stationary] river vegetation. The film or in-river vegetation can therefore be thoroughly examined, understood and interpreted at that particular instant in time. The "Frozen Frame" does not record what came before, or what will come after.

When a researcher studies a particular site along a river, what do the results of that freeze-frame investigation represent? It may of course be obvious, perhaps because a dredger passed through last week taking all the vegetation with it. Such a catastrophe can usually be seen and the event removed from any analysis. However, it is more likely that the actual reason for the lack of vegetation or different vegetation to that forecast, is far less obvious.

Long-term, of course, there must be change with climate change: at the extreme, when most of Britain was covered by ice some 10,000 years ago, the vegetation under that ice was not what is there today—without the ice and with an equable climate! But what about lesser time periods of 5, 15, 50 or 150 years ago? For how long has the vegetation remained stable? Unfortunately there is a lack of recorded history so this small book will summarise some of what is available, but its main aim is to inform, encourage, and pave the way for new interest.

Everyone fixes their own reference data. When someone studies a river site for the first time that is the reference vegetation and condition which that person will use life-long. "It is as it was in 1995. It is worse quality than in 1995. It improved 1995 to 1998 but has deteriorated since", etc.. This setting of one's own references is inevitable, but must be recognised when interpreting changes.

The first serious study of River Plant Ecology in England was by Butcher (1927, 1930). Meanwhile, and earlier, the Saprobic System was developed on the Continent. (The Saprobic System measures water quality—specifically the capacity of a water body to self-regulate and degrade organic matter.)

Much British and European field research carried out in the 1970s and 1980s added more British data. Several methods for recording vegetation have been devised over the years, some scientific, others by enthusiastic amateurs. Any recording method should be valued within its own parameters and all results should be taken into account. A striking example was an overheard conversation between junior colleagues, one favouring this author's method (1982), the other that of Holmes (1983). It got heated. If either had bothered to consult, they would have learnt that Holmes had been funded by the Conservancy Council, so rare plants on river banks were vital. I was funded by a Pollution Agency where rare bank plants—not being touched by polluted water—were irrelevant. Such unnecessary conflicts!

Most regrettably, in around 1995 (starting 1990 and spreading) river vegetation over much of the populous parts of Britain went into collapse. Diversity went down, quantity went down and the Government and authorities were quite unworried. The worst catastrophe known to British river vegetation had gone almost unstudied. There are indeed records from 1995 onwards, but using different methods for only a few rivers and with negligible link up. This is a major snag of computer work. When the papers always sat around, they might or might not be considered important, but all concerned knew they did exist. What has been dropped off computer files did "never exist".

This is not really the place to discuss recording methods, except to say that there have been some catastrophes. It is unfortunate that at the time much data was never recorded properly and was therefore lost to science, even though it was obvious that a collapse had happened. As long as the observer is conscientious, all methods are valid within their own parameters, and it ill-becomes any fieldworker—still less any on-line modeller—to dismiss such results as without value. A good example is this author's clear memory of sheets of white Water crowfoot (*Ranunculus*) flowers in early summer in the late 1950s at a site on the River Lark, Suffolk. Sheets so dominant, whether or not other species were abundant, means good conditions for *Ranunculus*, and so a good habitat. By 1989 there were no such sheets, and they have been absent since. But they, so their preferred habitat, were there, even if a modelled paper later says nothing is known, and that there never was *Ranunculus*.

PLANTS CHANGE

It is easy to overlook the truism that "PLANTS ARRIVE, GROW, MATURE AND DIE". A plant may be an "annual" living for only a few weeks, but in that time it becomes established, flowers, and bears fruit. At the other extreme it may be like the Common reed (*Phragmites australis*) whose underground stems (rhizomes) go on growing (dying at the back) for an estimated 1,000 years or more.

No vegetation is therefore, in the exact sense, stable. A Reed bed may look the same as it did ten years ago; so may a "sheet" of Water crowfoot, but they will not be the same individual shoots, leaves or flowers. This year's flower is unlikely to be in the exact same place as that of last year. (Fig. 3). In Britain, each reed lives for one season, growing up in spring from the rhizome tip and dying back in autumn.

Figure 4 shows pictures of reed-growth in consecutive years.

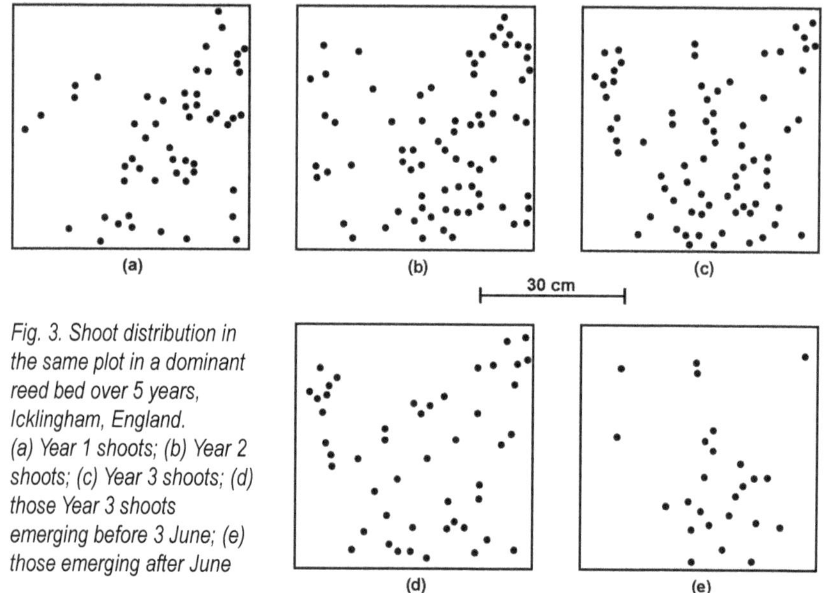

Fig. 3. Shoot distribution in the same plot in a dominant reed bed over 5 years, Icklingham, England. (a) Year 1 shoots; (b) Year 2 shoots; (c) Year 3 shoots; (d) those Year 3 shoots emerging before 3 June; (e) those emerging after June

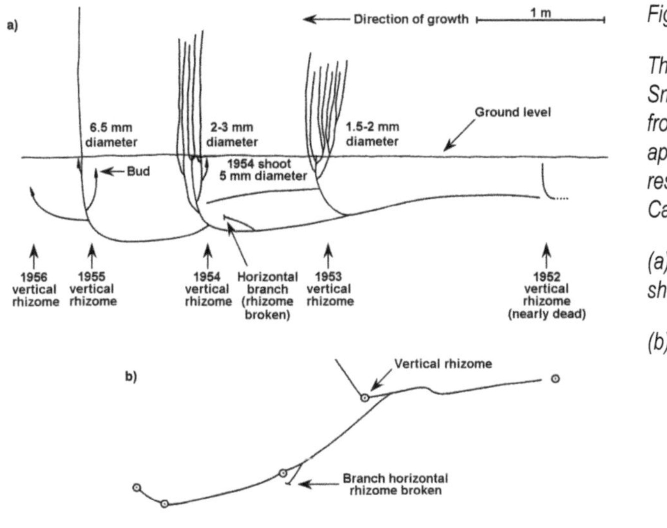

Fig. 4.

The Growth of a Reed. Small Phragmites *plants from dry fen, with strong apical dominance and restricted growth, Cavenham, England*

(a) Vertical plan (all aerial shoots of the same year

(b) horizontal plan

By and large the longer the subtending rhizome of the reed, the larger the reed: so in later years the "side reeds" of this years's new long-rhizomal reed become smaller, and also are closer. So a pattern develops. And this is the above-ground pattern! The rhizomes below ground also grow and their pattern changes by the year. But does that matter? Here comes another psychological factor: what we see, matters. What we cannot see, matters less or not at all. This author first started research on wetlands; it was not for another dozen years that I switched to rivers and for the first time started to wonder what happened to the water I watched disappearing down the sink! True, however deplorable. And you? Out of sight, out of mind. (More deplorable, of course, in me, as I was already an ecologist working in wet places!)

So, what about these changing patterns? If river vegetation changes, it alters *from* vegetation of some kind, *to* that of another kind, or becomes less, or none at all. There are streams with no obvious plant life, which look quite good, such as cascades and waterfalls, creeks on sticky unstable mud, various hot sulphur springs (with much algae, but no higher plants).

Most rivers, though, do have vegetation. If this is well-developed, there will be an emergent fringe of taller and shorter species (above water), a water-supported fringe inside it on the river edge, and underwater species usually down to a depth of about 1.2m. There could be between 9 and 19 species in a 25m reach of river—except, of course, where the river is, for example, shaded, has fast-flowing whitewaters, no shallow water, or no wetland edge.

Good river vegetation means that many species are present. Each plant species looks different and is different. It has different flowers, leaves, stems and roots. It is recognisably different. As well, it has a different habitat: some species grow best in shallow water, some in deeper water, some in very slow flowing water, others in faster flow, some have long, deep roots, others have short curly ones. Sometimes just looking can tell the habitat (see the fourth published book in the River Friend Series entitled, *INTERPRET—What do Plants Tell us?*). A plant with large, round floating leaves is not best adapted to whitewater, nor is one with frail, underwater floppy parts to growing out of the water.

In Britain there are some 130 macrophytes, or aquatic plants, which grow well in rivers. Anyone recognising about 70 can make a fairly reliable diagnosis for a habitat, provided several species are present. There are also Bryophytes (mosses and liverworts) and large algae.

Plants in good habitat conditions are healthier than those which are not, which usually means a larger and often longer-lived population. For instance, if a larger plant shoot on the river bed is growing into swifter flow near its tip, it is more likely to be washed off than shorter plants, the roots of both plants being equal. A damaged plant, though, may still be able to "live out" its natural span. It is easier for an established plant to continue in conditions which have become poor, than to re-invade (with young and vulnerable plants trying to establish in unsatisfactory surroundings). This is the way non-disastrous vegetation changes happen. When existing plants die and no longer exist in a place (which is often after about a year, but can be spread over a longer period of time) they are largely replaced by species which are better adapted to the new conditions.

THE HABITAT CHOOSES THE SPECIES is a principle worth remembering! But like all ecological statements it is not quite true: the habitat chooses, but only from those species whose propagules (which could be its fruit, seed, bulb, rhizome, winter bud, or stem fragment) are available! It is easy to think the plant chooses—but the plant's choice is very limited.

CHANGING COMMUNITIES

River Lark, Temple Bridge, Suffolk (Bridge is no longer there)

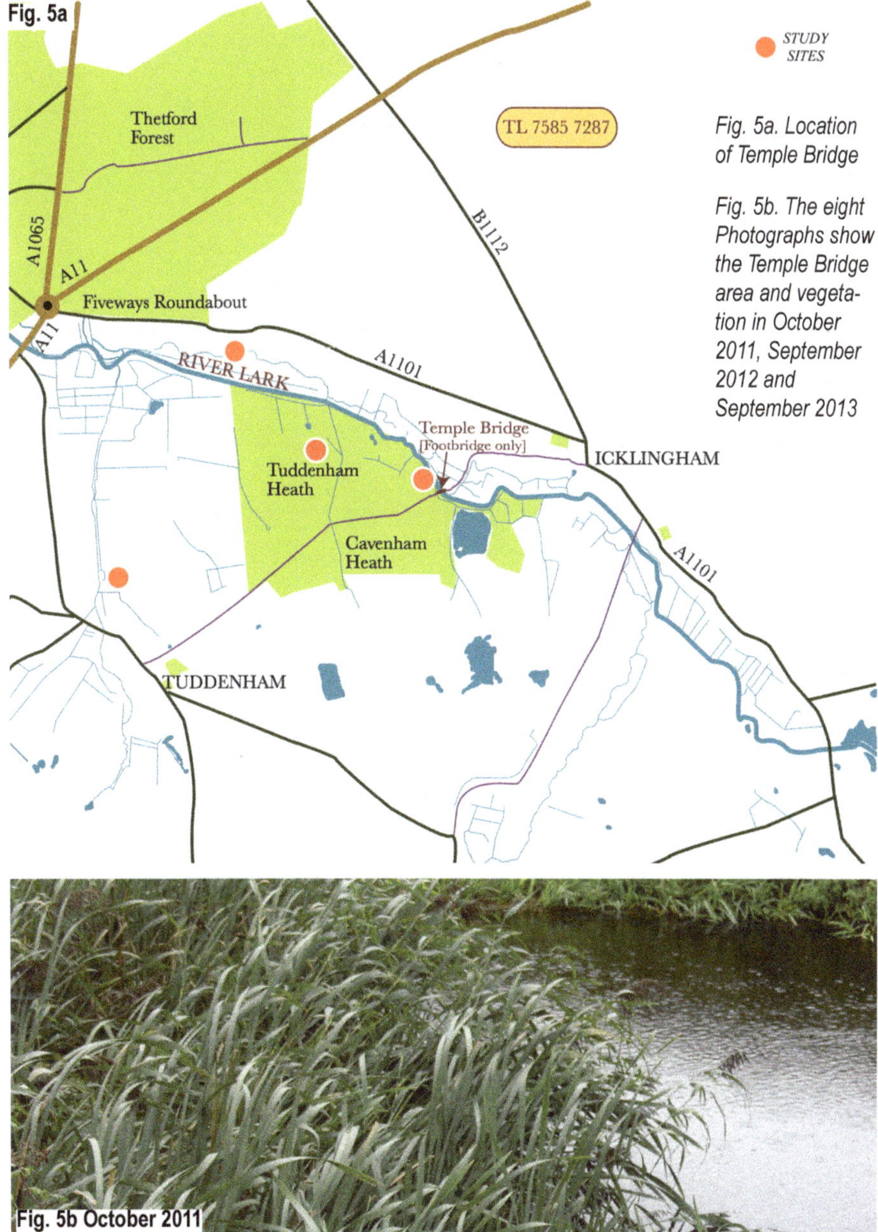

Fig. 5a. Location of Temple Bridge

Fig. 5b. The eight Photographs show the Temple Bridge area and vegetation in October 2011, September 2012 and September 2013

September 2012

September 2013 (6 photographs)

This river is unusual in that the vegetation has been watched, intermittently, from 1930 to 2014. The loss of individual species has been huge, though that of cover, and biomass, little. The water depth and flow have not changed much since 1950, nor, probably, before that, so the collapse must be attributed to other factors (*see Table 1 at the end of this book*).

In 1930 there was a worry about pollution from a sugar beet factory upstream. The large amount of *Potamogeton pectinatus* (Fennel pondweed, see Fig. 9b) shows this worry was justified; but of course was nothing compared with the agrochemical, domestic, hard surface, and other pollution which came later.

Worthy of note are:

(a) Short fringing herbs

Figure 6 shows two examples of Short Fringing Herbs, (a) *Mentha aquatica* (Water mint); (b) *Mimulus guttatus* (Monkey flower).

LOSS

Short fringing herbs grew well on the steep sides of the river in 1930 but, in similar physical conditions, they were absent in 2010. Root development is worse in pollution—so shoots (of the same size) are washed out more easily.

Fig. 6 (a) **(b)**

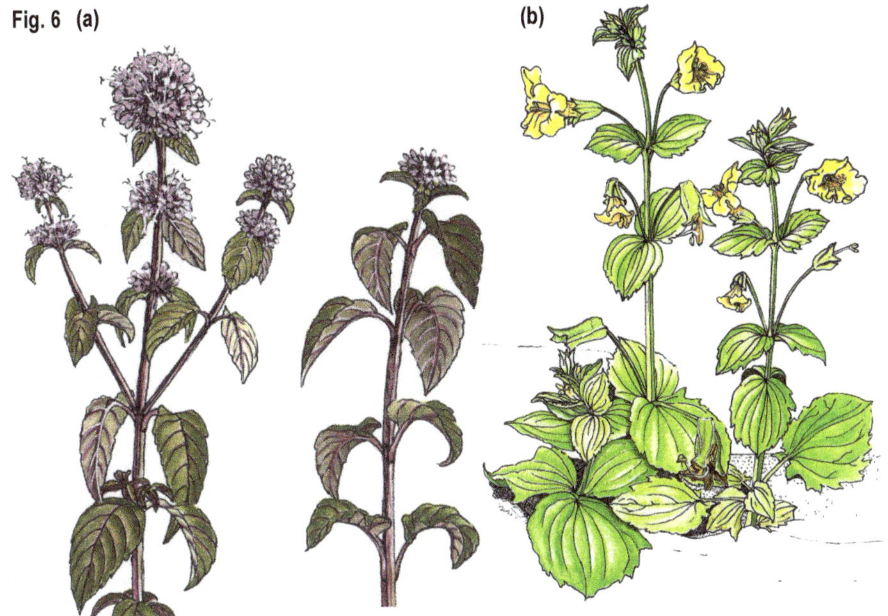

(b) Ranunculus fluitans (River Water crowfoot)

Fig. 7. *Ranunculus fluitans* (River water-crowfoot).

GAIN and LOSS

In 1930, ***Ranunculus*** was present, dominant in the 1950s, and restricted to hard edges from 1970 to 1985, where the curly roots could attach to stones in the bed and curl round firmly. In 1995 there was none. This would partly be due to earlier dredging removing the hard surface of the river bed. A small portion was left, and when *Ranunculus* grew beyond and outside this, it would be washed away by the next severe storm flow. So, *Ranunculus* increased between the 1930s and the 1950s, near-collapsed by the 1970s, and had completely gone by the 1990s. What features led to this? Water loss? Evidence of this being the primary cause of the loss is scanty. Some feature making a bud grow or not has been each of significant, minor, and absent.

In the 1970s, in most of the bed with under *c*.1m water depth, there were many species present. At the side was small (shrunken) *Ranunculus fluitans* firmly attached to consolidated gravel, obviously growing out from this. The roots cannot anchor well in soft soil, so if growth was poor, shoots small, or plants young, those plants would be washed off in the next storm. If given more time (and health), root wefts develop, and these partially consolidate the soil, so the plants are less easily washed off. This small patch, however, was effectively confined to the firm gravel, which was an old ford (by bridge). Only if conditions were better could the *Ranunculus* spread over the bed and dominate as it had once done; only if root anchorage was better or shoot buds could grow and form long shoots quickly, and swiftly replace those washed out by storms. Replacement-quick-growth is a necessity in order for species washed out to again flourish. It requires a good habitat, clearly, but what is that—depth, flow regime, major chemicals may be known, but there is much more to a habitat than that!

Ranunculus species in the rivers of much of Europe are the main river dominants. In good conditions the shoots run to several metres long, and have many roots, side shoots from rhizomes, or main shoots. *Potamogeton pectinatus*, minus most of the roots, is similar, but *Sparganium emersum* has a quite different habit, with leaves sprouting from the growing points on the rhizome. Dominant *Ranunculus*, in good communities, has up to a dozen or so other species growing alongside it, as well as over it, and in and under the plant's fringes. The other two species, when over-growing, tend to be monodominant with perhaps a "reedy" fringe, Fig. 8(a–d), consisting of tall monocotyledons such as *Acorus calamus* (Sweet flag), *Carex acutiformis* (Pond sedge), *Glyceria maxima* (Reed sweet grass), *Phragmites australis* (Common reed).

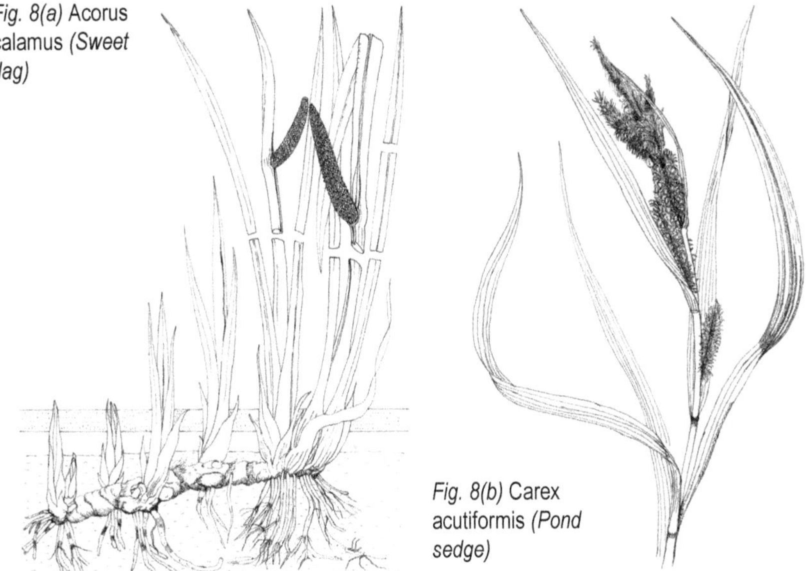

Fig. 8(a) Acorus calamus *(Sweet flag)*

Fig. 8(b) Carex acutiformis *(Pond sedge)*

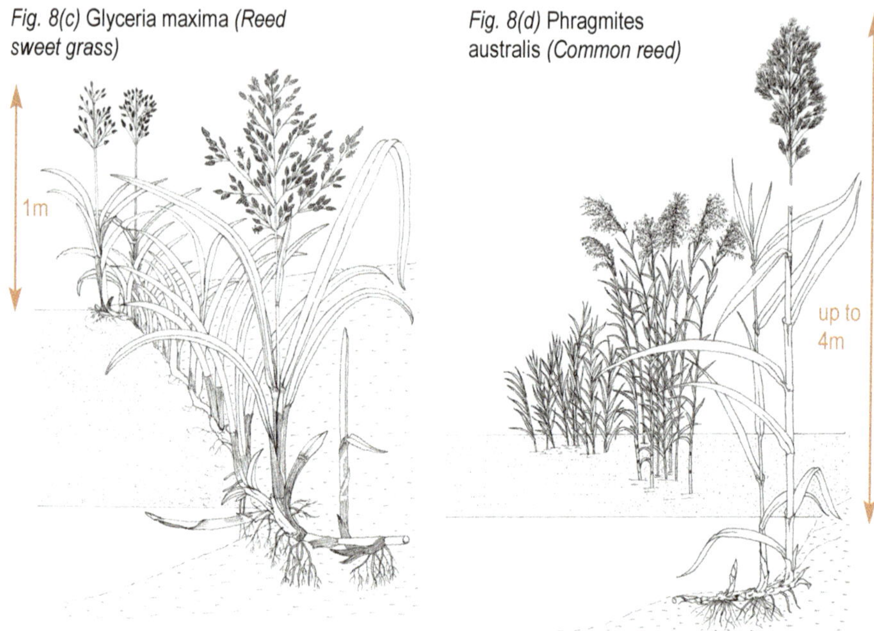

Fig. 8(c) Glyceria maxima *(Reed sweet grass)*

Fig. 8(d) Phragmites australis *(Common reed)*

It is interesting also that, in the rivers of North America in the 1970s and 1980s, *Ranunculus* species were both fewer and sparser, and that a range of mixed *Potamogetons*, none showing monodominant overgrowth, typically took their place. Why?

(c) Potamogetons (Pondweeds)

Fig. 9. (a) Potamogeton perfoliatus *(Perfoliate pondweed). (b)* Potamogeton pectinatus *(Fennel pondweed). (c)* Potamogeton natans *(broad-leaved pondweed). (d)* Potamogeton praelongus *(Long-stalked pondweed). (e)* Potamogeton pusillus *(Small/Lesser/Least pondweed. (f)* Potamogeton lucens *(Shining pondweed)*

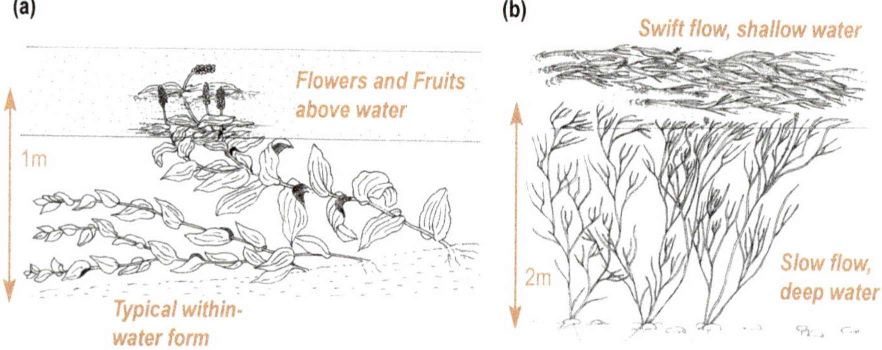

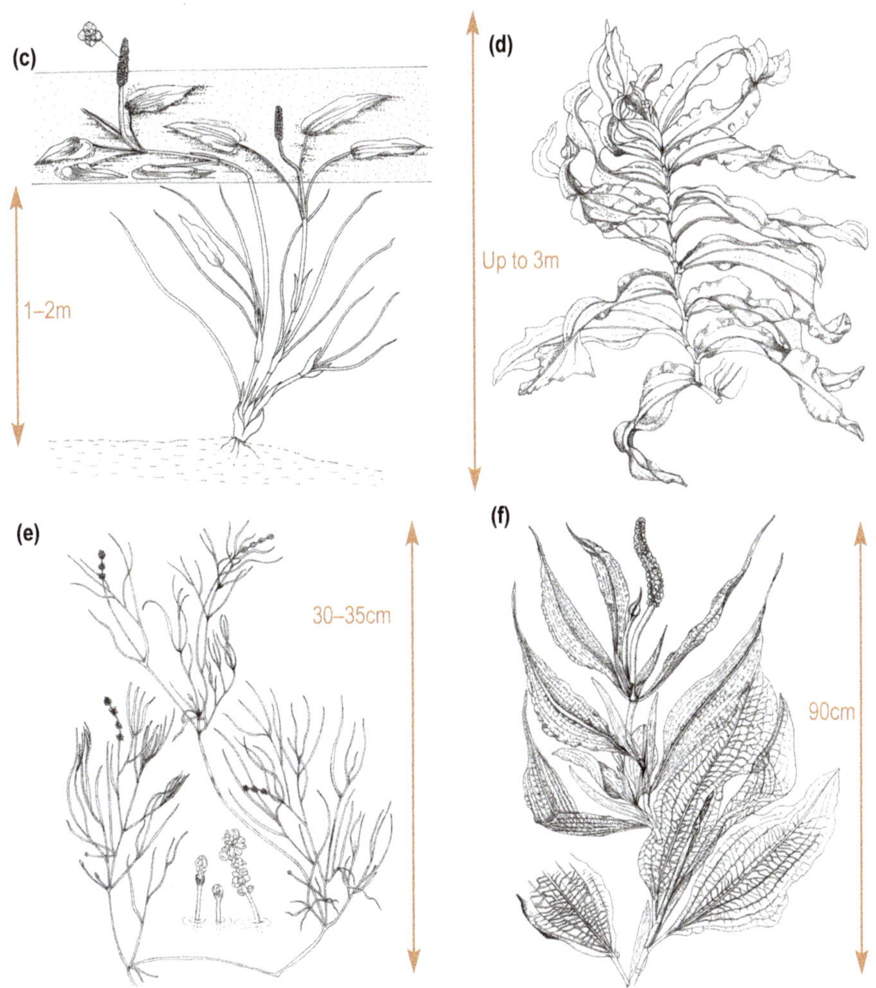

LOSS

In 1930, fine-leaved *Potamogetons* were common, and there could be several species present in study sites *c.* 25m long. By 1970 there were none at Temple Bridge. However, here in 1970 large-leaved *Potamogetons* (including *Potamogeton pectinatus*, which can be counted as large-leaved) were common. By 1995, all the *Potamogeton* species had gone, except *Potamogeton pectinatus* which was "monodominant", but this also disappeared before 2010. (*Potamogeton pectinatus* is usually diagnostic for domestic and some industrial pollution.)

This *Potamogeton* loss also occurred on the continent in Denmark and in Germany. The recorders attribute this to dredging the excess "weed" mechanically with large machines, instead of manually. This pulls the stems, so pulls on the roots, far more. And it shows, yet again, the sensitivity and selectivity of river plants.

Why? On the little evidence available, then, *Potamogeton* collapse is due, at least in part, to changing management. This still leaves the two-stage *Potamogeton* loss in England with even less explanation! What happened between 1930 and 1970 that removed most fine-leaved species? What happened between *c*. 1980 and 1995-ish that removed other large-leaved species but allowed, in the rivers studied, *Potamogeton pectinatus* over-growth, it becoming much larger? What happened between then and 2006 in these sites to make *Potamogeton pectinatus* vanish and be replaced by *Sparganium emersum* (strapweed), also large, vigorous and dominant?

When a good mixed community of aquatic plants turned to dominant *Potamogeton pectinatus*, did the other species get smaller, or just vanish? And did this happen all at once or over several years? When huge amounts of *Sparganium emersum* replaced the very large *Potamogeton pectinatus* plants, how did that happen? Sadly, the questions remain unanswered.

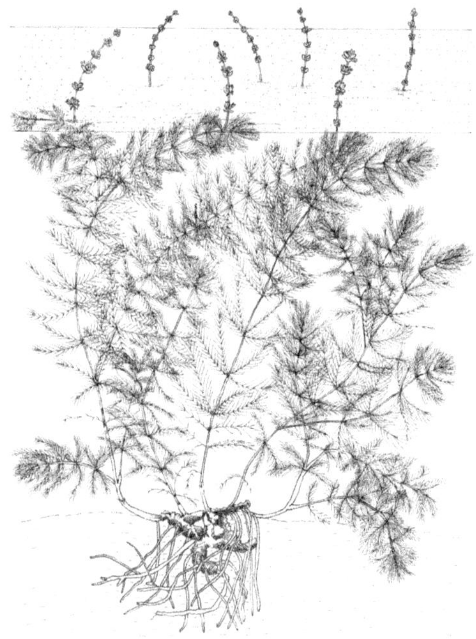

Fig. 10 Myriophyllum spicatum *(Water milfoil). The stems of this plant emerge from root crowns, whose white roots are fragile, smooth and hairless*

Potamogeton pectinatus can dominate in deep silt and slow flow downstream. In some years it was monodominant, in others, mixed in. Similarly, this can be true of *Myriophyllum spicatum* (Water milfoil, Fig. 10) and *Potamogeton perfoliatus* (see Fig. 9a), as both can be of similar size and habit. The density of *Potamogeton pectinatus* depends, indirectly, on the flow of the water, but more directly on how many winter buds (turions) or fruits are washed down to a suitable habitat in which they can grow. In spring, young plants, growing from propagules, can be fairly dense on the silt, and indeed also on the softer mixed substrate upstream. In both these, the young plants are easily eroded by storm flow, and when storms in May are frequent and severe, hardly any plants are likely to survive upstream, though they can if embedded in the deep silt downstream. If, though, storm flow is little, then *Potamogeton pectinatus* can become nearly co-dominant with, for example, *Sparganium emersum* or *Sagittaria sagittifolia*, as well as being dominant downstream.

If one species could be said to control the aquatic vegetation community (1960s to 1990s), it would be *Potamogeton pectinatus*. Other species grow well, or very well, depending on the flourishing of *Potamogeton pectinatus* and on the incidence of spring storms. If conditions allow *Potamogeton pectinatus* to flourish more, as happened in the 1980s, the plants become much bigger, occupy more space, and do not allow other species to grow in between. It is possible that this might be foreseen—but who could foresee its later replacement by *Sparganium emersum*?

COLLAPSE

The collapse of species at Temple Bridge on the River Lark has been recorded better than most. This, though, means more, not fewer, questions on "How Things Work"! What is known about the timing of this particular collapse (or rather, the absence of expected vegetation)? With so many questions remaining unanswered, it is sad that previous surveys in Britain have proved inadequate. European records, however, show that there was a collapse in the early 1980s in SW France, where, over a whole swathe, river vegetation was almost absent, and the water was not clear. At the same time in W France there was another swathe where vegetation was "more poorly" than might have been expected (both in species and quantity). In the 1990s, the unpublished 1970s surveys carried out by Mrs M.P. Everitt in W and SW France were repeated, and recorded that the vegetation had collapsed—suffice it to say that species and cover had both dropped alarmingly.

QUESTIONS

France, in the 1970s, was experimenting with manure slurry from sewage treatment plants, and was using it on a large scale. England had a collapse starting around the mid-1990s, and later. England's river-water levels dropped drastically, but did the same apply to France? Roads, and construction increased, but proportionately to land surface (catchment size), there was no noticeable drop in France. In Britain, the distribution and amount of the collapse varied. So what did happen? More unanswered questions!

(d) Sparganium emersum

Fig. 11. *Sparganium emersum* (Strapweed, Unbranched bur-reed).

GAIN and LOSS

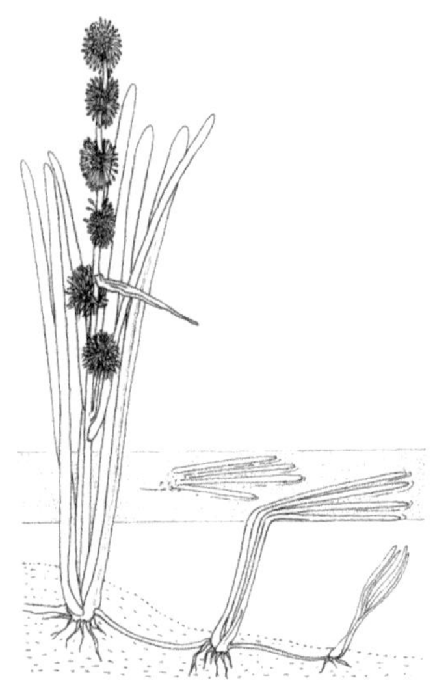

Near Temple Bridge *Sparganium emersum* became monodominant in 2009. *Potamogeton pectinatus* disappeared—at least in part. Up to about 1995, the vegetation pattern had changed only within small limits since 1930, and *Sparganium emersum* was small, generally sparse, and certainly unable to smother over other species such as the *Potamogetons*. In 2010, however, in *Sparganium emersum* rivers, *Potamogetons* were absent or restricted to, for example, small edge areas which for some reason had not been penetrated by the *Sparganium emersum*. The plants of 2009 were really flourishing, at least twice the size of those of the 1970s. A little fringe was present on the edge, but no other macrophytes were present (Fig. 12).

In the 1990s, *Potamogeton pectinatus*, in this reach, was large and flourishing, and *Sparganium emersum* was absent. By 2013, *Sparganium emersum* was less, and other species were coming back. Fringing herbs re-appeared on a "landslip bank" (with open habitat) (Fig. 13).

GAIN

If we now hark back to dominance and size, the River Lark is by no means the only river where *Sparganium emersum* doubled or trebled its leaf size, spreading vigorously over a river bed to become the dominant or monodominant species, where previously it had been small and sparse. Habit changes with this change. Being so much larger, the leaves are arranged longwise down the river, piled on each other instead of being a small, fan-like arrangement scattered at the side of the river, out of the main flow. The

Fig. 12. Monodominant Sparganium emersum, *no fringing herbs (2011)*

Fig. 13. Less Sparganium emersum, *and vegetation fringe on far bank, next to grazed meadow (2013)*

vigorous shoots flourished right across the bed of the River Lark and similar rivers such as the River Cam in W Cambridge. This stretch of the River Cam used to have a "clay-mix" vegetation, which included good *Sparganium emersum* with *Nuphar lutea* (yellow water lily, see Fig. 20) floating over. The other species then became very sparse. Where the river depth reached over 2m, even large *Sparganium emersum* leaves could not reach the surface, so an underwater meadow developed with the floppy *Sparganium emersum* leaves waving 1m down below the surface of the water—without a top covering of *Nuphar lutea*, for which, in the water, there was ample space. This is another example of diversity collapse, and *Sparganium emersum* becoming vigorous and dominant. Another vegetation collapse indeed, but how and why? Again, so many questions remain unanswered!

(e) Mixed Vegetation

LOSS

The texture in the centre of the river bed was patchy in the 1970s. The patches of firm but less consolidated gravel than the *Ranunculus* area bore *Oenanthe fluviatilis* (River water-dropwort) and *Potamogeton crispus* (Curled pondweed). These two plants also have curly root wefts (like *Ranunculus*) and anchor better in less firm substrate. They can grow well in a "mosaic", and at Temple Bridge were the same sort of size as the *Ranunculus*. Whatever allowed *Ranunculus* to flourish and dominate did not, in Europe, do the same for *Oenanthe fluviatilis* and *Potamogeton crispus*. In Europe, these can certainly grow larger than in Britain, but do not monodominate.

Also at this site were intermediate substrates of mixed grain, softer than the patchy river bed mentioned above, and with enough stones to still give stability. Two common species were present: *Sagittaria sagittifolia* (Fig. 14, Arrowhead) and *Sparganium emersum*. Both these plants have straight roots which anchor by growing deep down—not by curling round stones at the surface. The amount of *Sparganium emersum* was less than half what it was 25 years later, so it was unable to shade and smother other species.

(f) Discussion

To discuss in depth the general patterns in different types of riverscape, and the effects of various man-made impacts on river systems, is beyond the scope of this little book. However, the above points, taken together, illustrate some

Fig. 14. Sagittaria sagittifolia *(Arrowhead)*

important features. It is good to have a mixed vegetation community, nicely patterned with a pattern that can be understood. A plant mosaic in a river may, amongst commonly growing species, also have small associates, such as species kept small by, for example, fast flow, storm flow, grazing by animals, even calcium-dominated water.

Between this and the lands of collapse was a whole range of communities. By and large the more populous areas with higher and resultant impact, the worse the collapse.

Rather surprisingly mid-Wales was worse than expected: but added "manure", and farming, have both degraded agricultural soil, even up in the mountains. And, even though much money has been put into them, the Great Chalkstreams of Hampshire (the Rivers Test, Itchen and Avon) and smaller ones in Cambridgeshire, Yorkshire, and SE England, show that aquatic diversity and quantity are both down and that the water level is very low.

Why? Perhaps a good research project? Look at John Constable's picture of the River Avon at Salisbury, *c*. 1820 (Fig. 15), and see the *Ranunculus* filling the river and occupying as much space as it can, and then say there is no change. But, sadly, it had greatly changed by 1970, and even more, since.

Fig 15. Constables Water Meadows (painted either 1820 or 1829). Note plenty of water and aquatic plant species, with room to grow. Photograph, courtesy of the V&A Collection - given by John Sheepshanks, 1857

River Rhee (Harston and Barrington), Cambridgeshire

The River Rhee, a tributary of the River Cam, rises in Chalk, and flows mainly over Chalk and Alluvium (deposits of silt—sand, etc., especially in river valleys and delta—left by water flowing over land which is not permanently submerged). Various of its upper brooks are "proper Chalkstreams", though at the two sites examined here (Barrington and Harston), the river was Chalk-mixed in type.

Figures 16 and 17 show the location of the field sites of Harston and Barrington respectively.

*Fig. 16 Location of Field Site at Harston. a View from Bridge looking downstream, River Rhee at Harston 2011 (*Ranunculus *left and centre, short bushy fringing herbs on left,* Sparganium emersum *front right), b 2012 (*Sparganium emersum *has taken over; a few sprigs of* Ranunculus *top centre, fewer small fringing herbs as bank vegetation has grown over). c(i) 2013 June* Ranunculus *growing well, and small fringing herbs returned (bank vegetation cut back); inset same patch July 2010. c(ii) September 2013, one tiny patch of* Ranunculus *top centre (ringed in red),* Sparganium emersum *dominating, but short fringing herbs crowding into mid-stream from the left; nettles and sprawling False bindweed on the right*

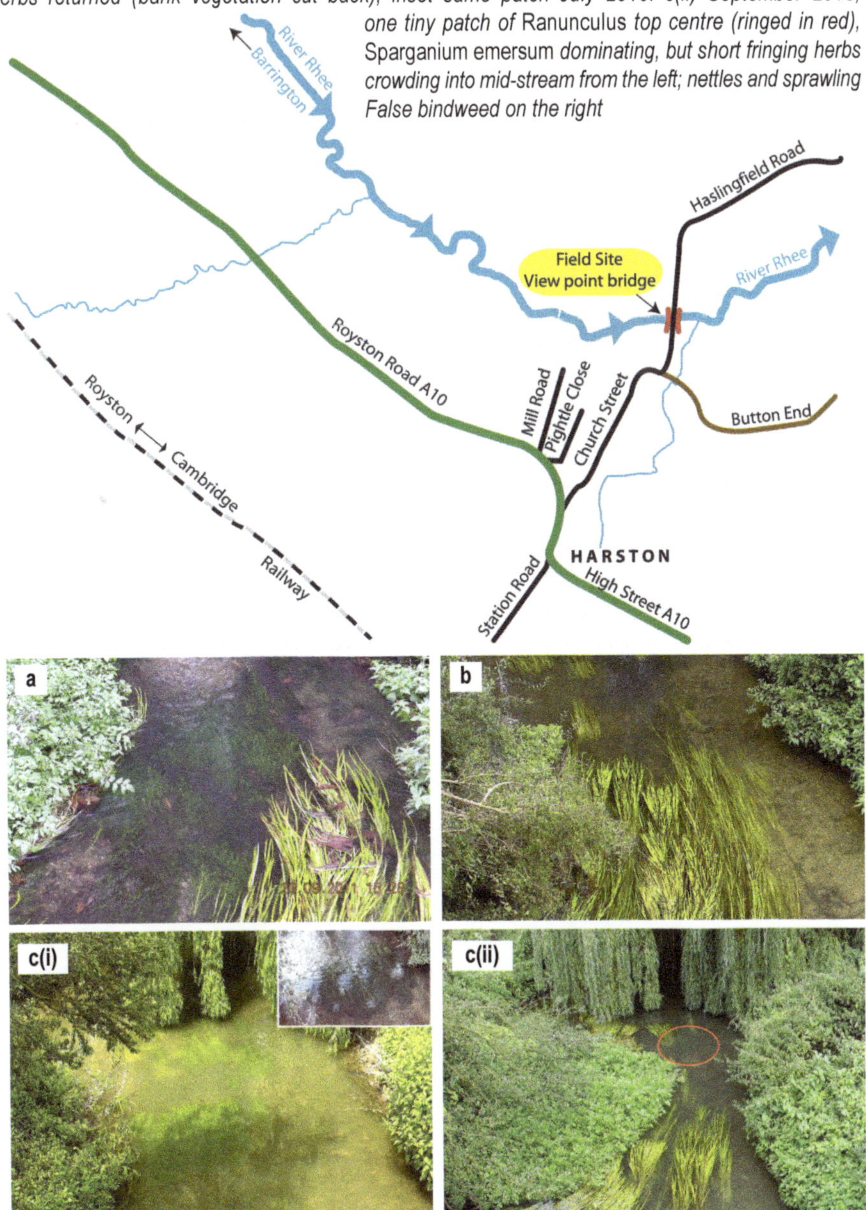

Fig. 17 Location of Field Site at Barrington. a(i) River Rhee at Barrington 2011, looking downstream, near bridge, water cloudy with sparse Sparganium emersum*; a(ii) further upstream short, bushy fringing herbs and more* Sparganium emersum*, note frothy scum top left. b 2012 note short fringing herbs gone and replaced by tall reedy plants. c 2013* Sparganium emersum *still dominant, less fringing herbs, a lot more shade from trees and bank vegetation*

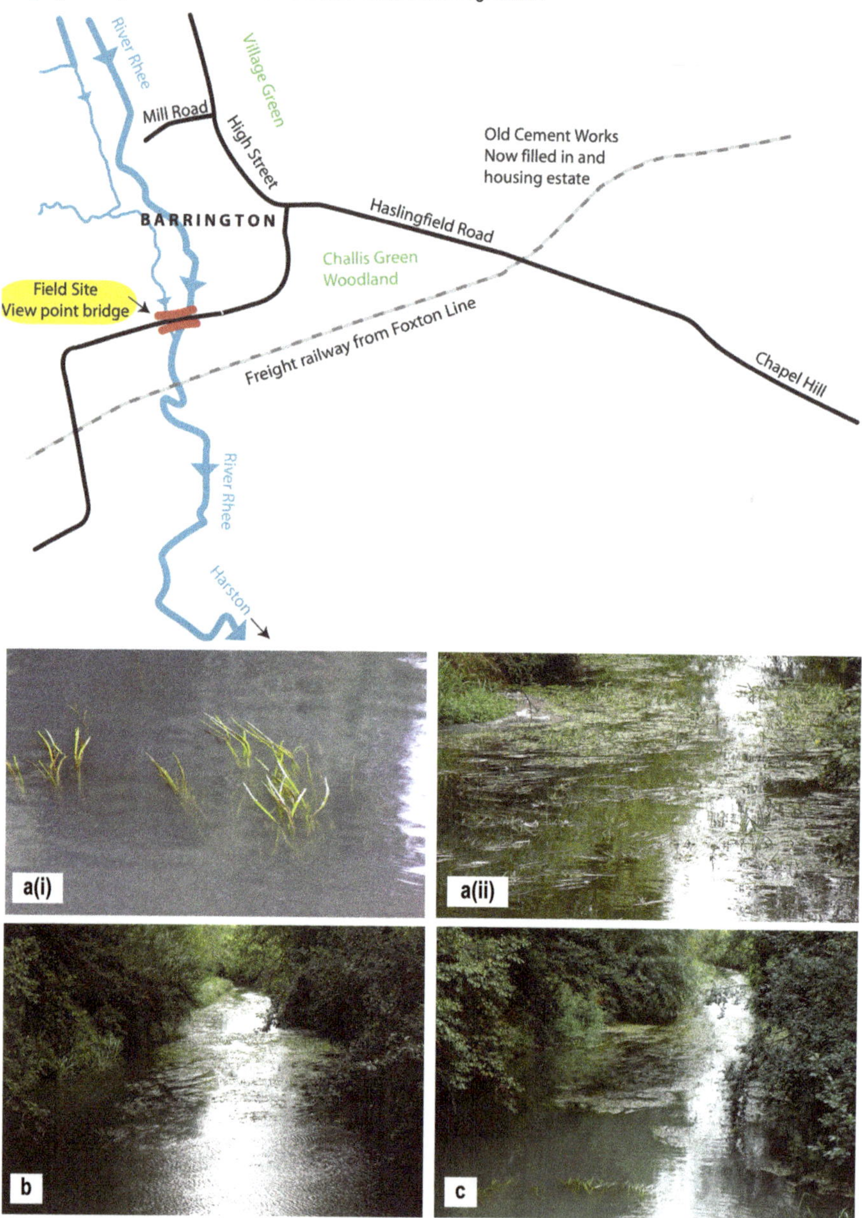

USED TO BE

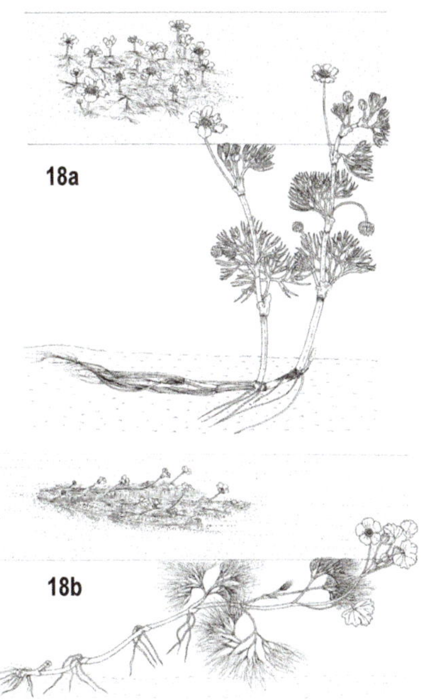

The Barrington site, which is a man-made channel, raised up above the level of the valley and the River Rhee, to give height to power a mill, was studied intensively from 1969 to 1985 when its vegetation assemblage was stable. Downstream of a watergate the flow was silted and slow with *Potamogeton pectinatus* dominant and a few other species present. Upstream of the gate 30–50cm water flowed well over gravel, and out of heavy shade two species of *Ranunculus* (*Ranunculus trichophyllus*, short-leaved, Fig. 18a, and *Ranunculus penicillatus*, medium-length leaves Fig. 18b) grew well, with a few fringing herbs, such as *Veronica beccabunga* (water speedwell, Fig. 18c), scattered around. Upon closer inspection, it could be seen that the water was too shallow, the plants being crushed down within the water, and a low (under 50%) cover of vegetation indicated other damage as well (Fig. 18d).

It was thought that there was, so I was assured, no upstream pollution at this site, but the presence of pollution-tolerant *Potamogeton pectinatus* indicated that there may have been some effluent pollution.

Later I discovered there was a factory whose pollution had effectively been denied.

Anyway, this pollution meant that the *Ranunculus* was continuously soaked in moderately polluted and too shallow water, with polluted silt particles being dumped on the river bed between storms. No wonder growth was poor! However, growth was good enough for cutting, usually alternate years—the best-growing *Ranunculus* streams need cutting 3–5 times each summer (Fig. 19). Prevailing conditions did not permit spreading by rhizomes sideways or longways, so the community in this instance was merely maintained.

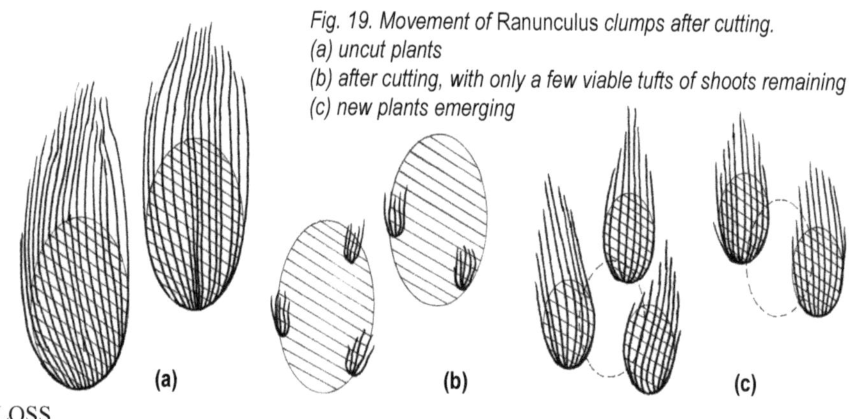

Fig. 19. Movement of Ranunculus *clumps after cutting.*
(a) uncut plants
(b) after cutting, with only a few viable tufts of shoots remaining
(c) new plants emerging

LOSS

In 2008, however, both *Ranunculus* and *Potamogeton pectinatus* had vanished ("collapsed"). Only a little tall "reedy" fringe remained along unshaded edges. The in-river vegetation once poor or sub-adequate, had now collapsed completely. Water was less, but still flowing.

Harston

USED TO BE

The next-downstream site at Harston gave further distance for self-purification from the factory, and *Ranunculus* grew fairly well (outside shaded places). Upstream, in light shade and slower, siltier flow, so did Yellow water-lily (*Nuphar lutea*, Fig. 20, September 2012), *Callitriche* spp. (Fig. 21) and *Sparganium emersum* (Fig. 22) (with quite large leaves (nutrient-rich, and not Chalkstream-size), Fool's watercress (*Apium nodiflorum*, Fig. 23), and other fringing and edge species. In the 1970s there were horses grazing downstream. *Ranunculus*, well-grown but also well-trampled, filled most of the stream.

Fig. 20. **a** Ranunculus *growing north of bridge in gravel bed with swifter flow.* **b** Nuphar lutea *growing south of bridge in silty water, submerged leaves just visible.* **c** Nuphar lutea *north of bridge (downstream) before* Ranunculus *patches, note* Sparganium emersum *(left), gravel bed, and swifter flow*

Fig. 21 (above). *Clumps of* Callitriche *crowded in silty shallow water*

Fig. 22 Sparganium emersum *with vigorous growth*

Fig. 23 (right). Apium nodiflorum *growing in silt at the water's edge*

LOSS

Whilst at Barrington the vegetation had certainly collapsed, at Harston upstream how should that be described? The species had moved away from those of a Chalkstream, but were still diverse and with good cover? "Collapse" in one sense, but not in another!

In the 1990s, a little unhappy, unhealthy *Nuphar lutea* appeared just downstream of the bridge, presumably having spread down. It looked as though the next storm would wash it away. Surprisingly, two decades on it was still there—but still small and unhealthy. So if water and flow return to what they were pre-1990, it would surely be washed out? If, though, the water slows or silt increases the *Nuphar lutea* is poised to take advantage of this and spread over such a habitat, and become dominant. Meanwhile it is just waiting, and will eventually be lost or develop as circumstances dictate. Upstream of the "poised" *Nuphar lutea* however, plants such as *Sparganium emersum* came, saw, and co-dominated: in water which had become less and was siltier.

Over the years the swift-running *Ranunculus* habitat decreased, the soil-plus-water was transitional. Depending on flow it could support either those species requiring a nutrient-rich habitat or the *Ranunculus* communities. In far too many places loss of water plus an increase in polluted, silty soil had caused the vegetation pattern to continually switch in this way—this is "partial" collapse.

THEORY

Ranunculus is the more nutrient-poor community. Why is this considered the better—or the worse—community? Firstly, the best "game" fishery (trout and salmon) rivers are those with *Ranunculus* growing in them—not those with *Nuphar lutea*—because game anglers will pay the most to fish them. So, simple economics dictates that *Ranunculus* rivers are the "best". Also these rivers are well looked after to promote and maintain the habitat for this multi-million pound industry. The coarse fishery rivers with *Nuphar lutea* rank lower. Secondly, agricultural crops used to be short of nutrients and were manured with all sorts of peculiar things (including pigeon-feet!). When powdered fertilisers became plentiful, they also ran off the land or sunk into it. The "fertilised" (nutrient-rich) groundwater and rising springs, with all their newly-gathered excess nutrients, flowed into the rivers causing the change in plant communities. It is the *Ranunculus* and lower-nutrient plant communities which are diminishing, and need—but do not get—some help, even in order to stay stable let alone to return to their previous state. Silt and clay carry more chemicals—solutes and particles—than do sand and stone. Consequently the lack of water reduces flow, dilutes less, so increases both nutrient and pollutant status, even if the actual chemical input is the same. So *Ranunculus* is the more important vegetation at this period—in the future, money, water or chemicals could change its status.

LOSS and GAIN (Harston)

Returning to the Harston site, the good *Ranunculus* downstream vegetation, growing well in the open, became shaded: which is a collapse, but a temporary one, with an easily-reversible cause. In 2008, the patch of *Ranunculus* near the (viewing) bridge had grown to 2m long in May spreading to 5m wide, which was adequate. By June, however, the patch had retreated, the shoots were a little over 0.5m and the patch size was roughly that of the winter. Blanket weed (*Cladophora glomerata*) had grown to much the same length as the *Ranunculus* but was spread over a larger area. Further deterioration followed, and in August *Ranunculus* shoots were only *c*. 10cm long, and were buried in short blanket weed (Fig. 24).

This was an undoubted collapse in 2008. However, next spring the *Ranunculus* was able to grow well, and store food in the rhizomes and stolons. But shoot growth and the growth of buds from the underground system stayed inside the winter patch (where they and the roots were anchored the most firmly). Why?

The future did not look good for *Ranunculus*! However, in 2009 there was the same burst of early growth as in 2008, but this year the *Ranunculus* continued to grow well with shoots several metres long, spreading over most of the stream width and competing successfully with *Sparganium emersum*—for that recently invasive plant was growing here also. Upstream in the *Nuphar* (slow, silted) habitat it was co-dominant with *Nuphar lutea*, with the usual "clay" associates: Arrowhead (*Sagittaria sagittifolia*), Canadian pondweed (*Elodea canadensis*), *Callitriche* spp. and at the fringes (almost too much) *Sparganium erectum*, *Apium nodiflorum*, and *Myosotis scorpioides* (Water-forget-me-not). Nine species in all. This high diversity (especially for a small stream) indicated that pollution, though obviously present, was not excessive (Fig. 25).

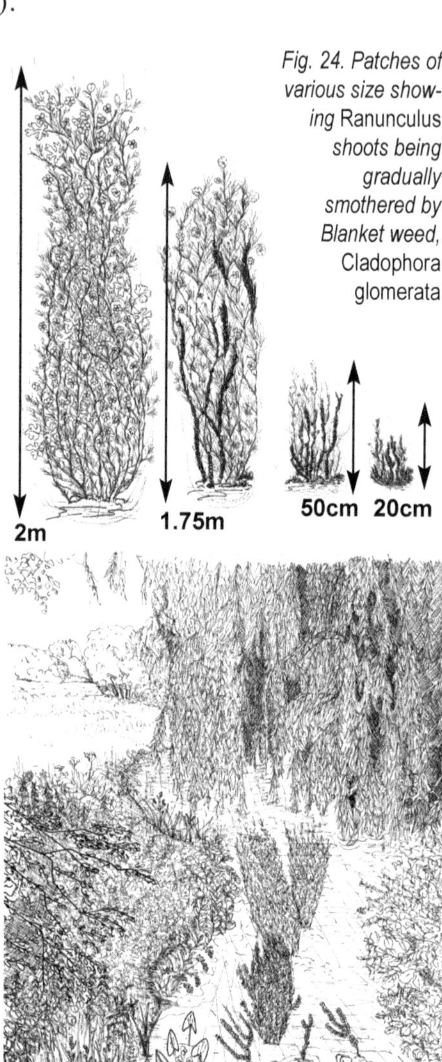

Fig. 24. Patches of various size showing Ranunculus *shoots being gradually smothered by Blanket weed,* Cladophora glomerata

Fig. 25. Typical habitat as described for 2009 at the Harston site

Sparganium emersum was present upstream and downstream, perhaps larger than "normal", but not excessively so. It spread downstream when the *Ranunculus* was not in the way, and retreated when that grew well. In about 1996 it seemed that *Nuphar lutea* and *Sparganium emersum* were replacing both the upstream slow (silty) area and the partly rippling shallower gravel (and silt) downstream section. Instead *Ranunculus* maintained itself (with difficulty) and *Sparganium emersum* became frequent or abundant, but also could not reach or maintain dominance—and most people think that plants grow happily together!

Chemical analysis is greatly needed! And many full-time researchers are wanted! A simple explanation for the *Ranunculus* "fiasco" in 2008 at the River Rhee Barrington site could be that perhaps sewage slurry was spread on the fields in May and was quickly—before it had time to be absorbed—washed into the river by a storm. But, sadly, no one was looking! But also, an optimistic point is that recent agricultural legislation (including new Farming Rules for Water which were introduced in April 2018) requires every farmer to work to similar standards and, for example, they are now "under a legal obligation not to pollute waterways or to cause a public nuisance through smell." So if farmers are beginning to "look", there is hope! Though not much. In early 2023, many reports said pollution was now much worse.

TUDDENHAM MILL STREAM, TUDDENHAM, SUFFOLK

HISTORY

This stream, like the Barrington site above, is a man-made channel, raised up above the level of the valley and Tuddenham stream, to give height to power the mill: which is still there. The mill stream was used for transport until early in the twentieth century. A horse pulled a barge up from the River Lark to just below the mill. A road crossed the stream, by a ford. To one side there was an earthen wharf, with a probably nineteenth century warehouse for storage. This is a common pattern. The most obvious place for water level to be adjusted was at the mill where water was raised in level so that it would turn the wheel more efficiently. Boats could pass the mill where the level was high. When the water was being ponded (impounded) for boats, wheeled traffic could pass across the ford. Once the mill was disused, the ford was replaced by a full-time road. Once barges were no longer towed up, the wharf became disused, and the mill house use changed—in 2020, a high-class hotel and restaurant.

The loss of a good, simple, piece of historic heritage, in 1970 (the restaurant was established in 1972), was still quite plain to see! This particular collapse was not inevitable. It came probably because none of those concerned realised what was present. The loss of irreplaceable historic heritage—its collapse—is as unfortunate as that of natural heritage. In fact it is often worse, since natural heritage may be left in part, or be restorable.

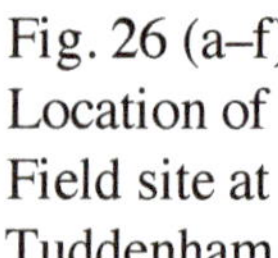

Fig. 26 (a–f) Location of Field site at Tuddenham

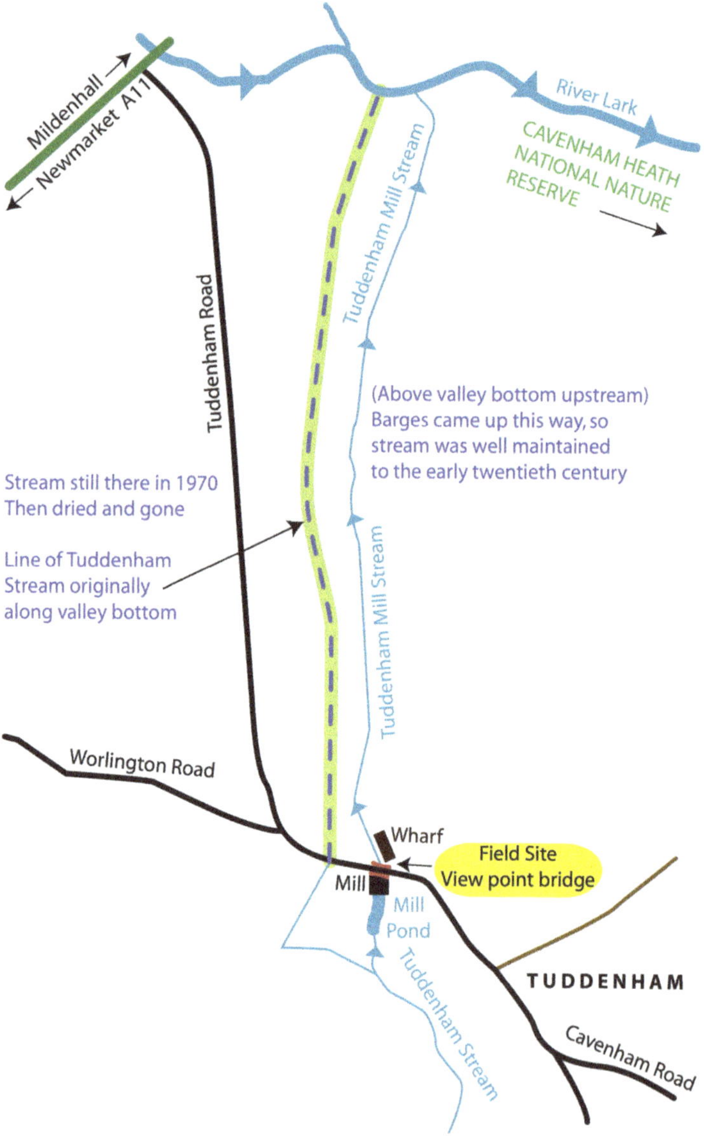

In 1989 the Tuddenham Mill Stream had long been disused for both power generation and transport, and consequently had little disturbance. The water was good, clear Chalk water from a spring a few kilometres upstream, which

Fig. 26 continued: **a** *An early photograph of Tuddenham Mill (date unknown) which shows the ford crossing and large pool.* **b** *Tuddenham Mill 2013 (high class hotel and restaurant). The water still runs under the mill and road to Tuddenham Mill Stream (left).* **c** *(2013) Tunnel running from the mill under the road. Archway shows very little water trickling over into the "pool", new growth of aquatic vegetation.* **d** *(2013) Pool showing active vehicular ford usage.* **e** *(2012) Pool showing pollution (oil and foam). Note small patch of young water cress growing on dry bank (encircled in red) and much Blanket weed in the shallow water surrounding it.* **f** *(2012) Archway to pool showing little water and scant fringing or aquatic vegetation—much Blanket weed*

had as yet received very little pollution. The *Ranunculus*, in *c*. 75cm water, was large and flourishing, most unusual for little brooks of this size at the time in England, but rather like Danish ones of the 1970s for instance (where such streams could even be well-known for salmon fishing). Diversity here, though, just like other English brooks this narrow, was unfortunately low.

In 1970 the dredgers moved in. The bed was lowered by up to 1m, which also meant losing the hard bed of the brook, together with all its plant propagules. This lowered the water depth to *c*. 30cm which is too shallow for this *Ranunculus* to grow. The stream bed was disrupted and became unstable. Water Parsnip *(Berula erecta*, Fig. 27), a characteristic species of Chalkstreams, disappeared after the dredging, but soon recolonised the edges, together with a little unhealthy *Callitriche* sp..

Fig. 27
Water parsnip
*(*Berula erecta*)*

After a decade or so, at the top of the old ford, the old stones formed a little stable pool area where *Ranunculus* (with its curly roots) could establish, but in such a small area shoots were small, and soon disappeared (Fig. 28).

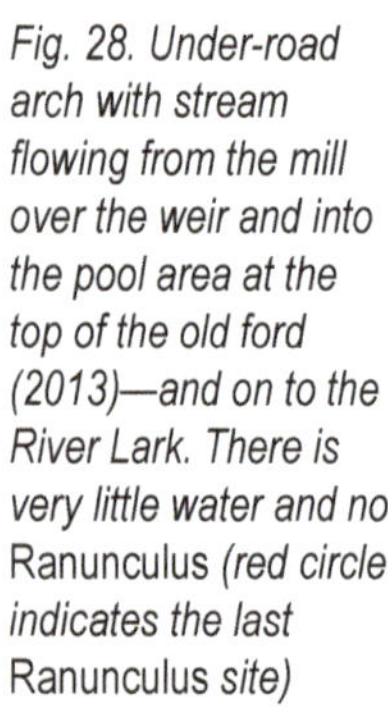

Fig. 28. Under-road arch with stream flowing from the mill over the weir and into the pool area at the top of the old ford (2013)—and on to the River Lark. There is very little water and no Ranunculus *(red circle indicates the last* Ranunculus *site)*

During the period 1970 to 2010 the stream bed, bank, and water were all "scrappy" and poor; aquatic vegetation was negligible.

DRYING UP, ALSO

Over this general area, licences for abstraction allowed the groundwater to be lowered. It is not known how far this has affected the lack of recovery. The licences, granted in the nineteenth or earlier twentieth centuries, were granted for local mostly field irrigation, but this was not specified, and—without an Act of Parliament—as population and water usage increased, water could be abstracted in huge quantities, and this has greatly affected the flood grasslands and "wild" wetlands.

River Great Ouse SW of Newport Pagnell

Fig. 29 (a–b) Site map North Bridge, River Great Ouse

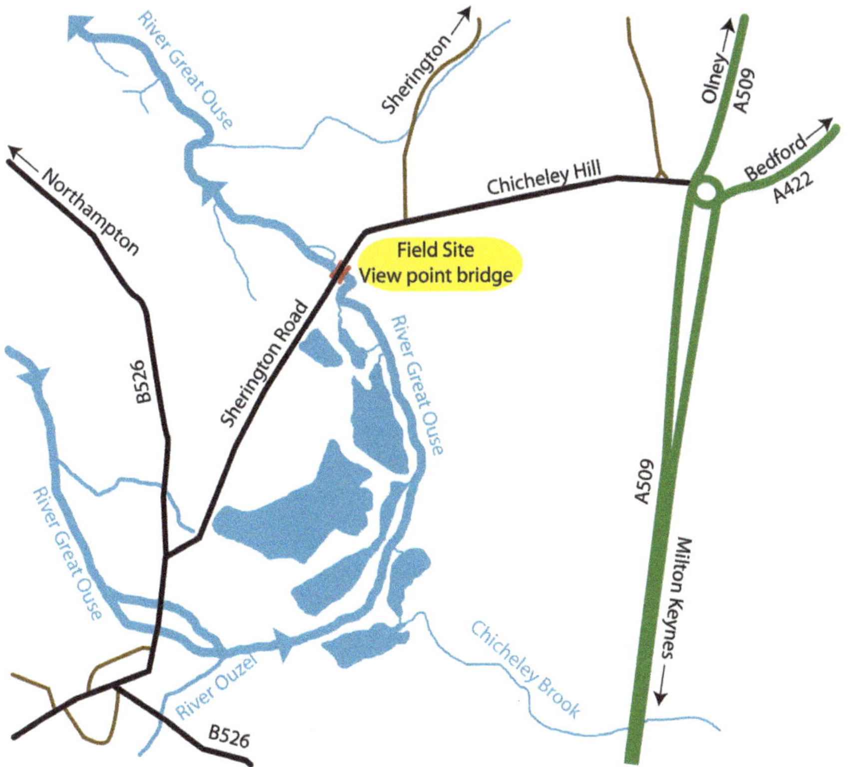

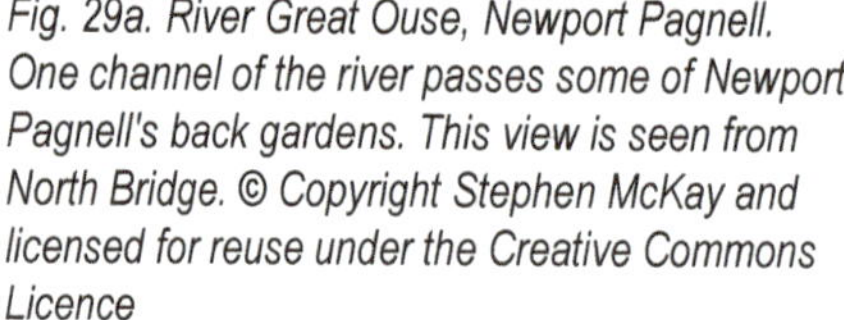

Fig. 29a. River Great Ouse, Newport Pagnell. One channel of the river passes some of Newport Pagnell's back gardens. This view is seen from North Bridge. © Copyright Stephen McKay and licensed for reuse under the Creative Commons Licence

Fig. 29b. River Great Ouse, Newport Pagnell Looking down from North Bridge to one channel of the River Great Ouse; the steps are part of Ousebank Gardens (© as for Fig. 29a)

This reach of river during the 1970s and 1980s was slow-flowing, silted, 0.5–1.5m deep in the main flow, with a good fringe of (mainly) tall emergents, and a good flora including abundant *Nuphar lutea*, frequent Clubrush or Bulrush (*Scirpus lacustris*), centre and fringing, with the usual associates, for example, *Sparganium emersum*, *Sagittaria sagittifolia* and *Apium nodiflorum*. It seemed to be a normal mainly clay East Midlands river, though the vegetation growth was excessive and dredging could be expected soon—in fact next summer!

DREDGING

Dredging did not just remove the silt and excess vegetation, it excavated so much that the water depth was only about 50cm on gravel with moderate flow, with transverse bars where the substrate was firmer. What with the dredging, and the water being so shallow, the *Nuphar lutea* had mainly gone, and that remaining was smaller, pulled over by the flow, and did not look healthy. That was as expected. The surprise was that *Ranunculus fluitans*, which had not been seen in the reach for at least a dozen years, was not only present, but covered *c*. 20% of the bed! The shoots obviously flourished, though they did not look healthy, and instead of being (as normal) several metres long, were barely over 0.5m. *Ranunculus fluitans* tolerates more nutrients than the more Chalkstream *Ranunculus*. Few other species were present (except for a narrow reedy fringe).

The vegetation had partly collapsed, the diversity had collapsed, the cover and biomass had gone down by some 75%. This was due to disturbance (dredging) altering the river bed shape and processes.

Dear Reader, SKIP THIS if you are reading to find out if communities change. Study it for its complexities if you need more…!

THE (ABERDEEN) RIVER DON, 1969–1991

Fig. 30 (a–e). Site Map River Don

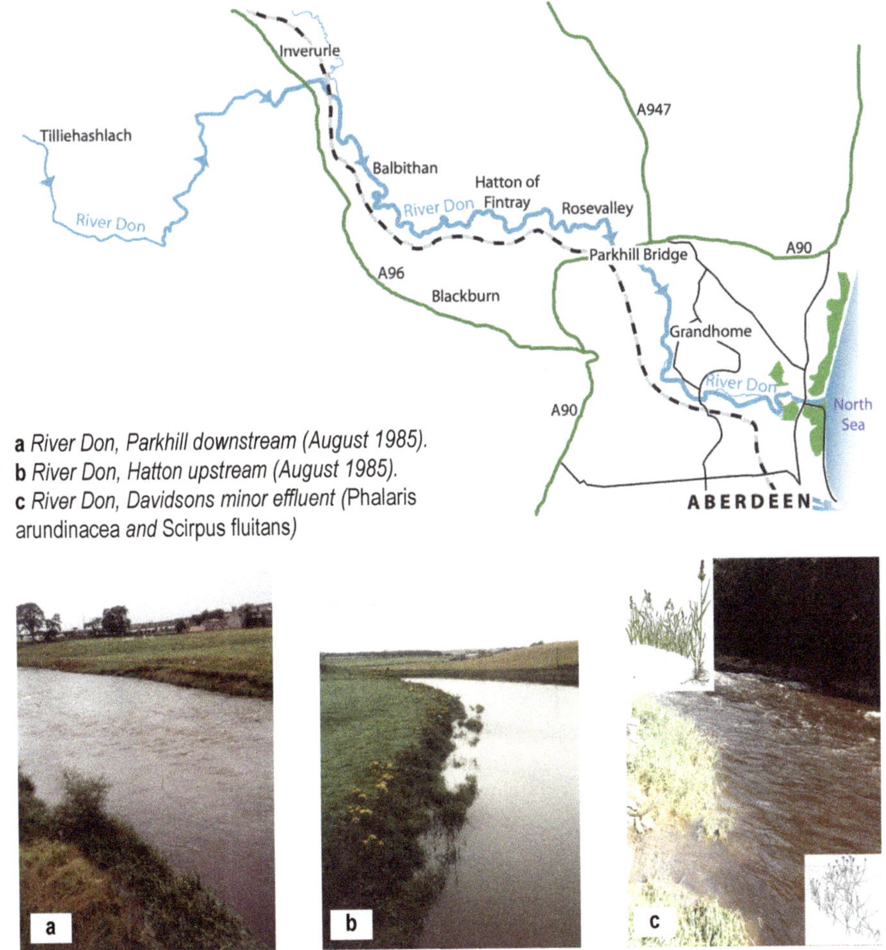

a *River Don, Parkhill downstream (August 1985).*
b *River Don, Hatton upstream (August 1985).*
c *River Don, Davidsons minor effluent (*Phalaris arundinacea *and* Scirpus fluitans*)*

Fig. 30 continued:

d *River Don at Tilliehaslach*

e *River Don, Grandhome (August 1986)*

THE SITE

This example is for a large part of a sizeable river, rather than a single site or short length. The river rises in resistant rock mountains, where bog peat leaches (and erodes) into the mountain tributaries, giving nutrient-poor vegetation, Downstream it flows through hills and agricultural lowlands before reaching its mouth at Aberdeen. The urban area by and near Aberdeen is increasingly being developed. The tale of the different chemical influences on the river plants, and their response, is illuminating.

Paper mills deal in paper: dead plant material. The effluent is this, plus processing and other chemicals, of which those of the upper mill have the greater variety and toxicity.

Above all this pollution is a site of really satisfactory vegetation—though the water is carrying effluent. This is the reference site for what follows. Next downstream is a site with adequate vegetation, suffering at times from too low a water level, and also from minor and increasing pollution from a tributary (more sewage fungus). Various streams—"airport" tributaries—bring in the new and increasing run-off pollution from that development. Even in 1981 this led to visible oil, in the River Don, and yellowed *Glyceria maxima* above the upper paper mill. From here down, the vegetation is limited in rapid bouldery reaches by water force, in deep slow reaches by depth, and recording may be hampered by water darkness or turbidity. Lack of an "a" rating is, by itself, no evidence of pollution.

The invertebrate community is adequate upstream. It shows a small drop in the airport streams region, a greater one with the paper mills and sewage works, and there is no proper downstream recovery. The index is worse on the south of the channel (upstream of the weir that causes complete water mixing). Most of the damage is from oxygen depletion. In the past, deposited solids and smothering sewage fungus were important, with minor toxicity. Macrophytes indicate the position of discharges, since they respond immediately to toxicity. Invertebrates responding primarily to oxygen shortage are necessarily worst where oxygen is least, some way below the discharge. Both water quality and invertebrate indices have improved in recent years.

DISCHARGES

The paper mills and airport streams discharge to the south bank, the sewage works, to the north. Point-source pollution spreads diagonally downstream, more mobile compounds moving first. So the upper mill has a simple diagonal poison-line from the discharge. The varied toxicities led, in the earlier years of the period (1981–1987) to a sharp drop in macrophytes (in a physically satisfactory reach of river). The lower mill has no such obvious pattern. Flow regime changes too much at the site for a diagonal line to show, and there is little obvious change in the channel vegetation anyway. By 25m or so below most effluents, there is cross-river mixing of (major!) pollutants toxic to macrophytes. It is different here for sewage fungus and invertebrates. In the days when sewage fungus was standard, particularly below the lower mill, it hugged its own south side until complete water mixing at a weir a kilometre or so downstream. Invertebrates followed the same pattern. Carbohydrates, suspended solids, and oxygen depletion are all important here. The fish populations have not been demonstrably affected.

SEWAGE FUNGUS

Sewage fungus occurs with suitable food, flow and temperature. Formerly it was rare above the paper mills, intermittent to the lower mill, excessive some way below that, and decreasing before the river mouth. In and about 1981, therefore, macrophyte quality decreased first, just by the upper mill, and was largely recovered by the mouth. In contrast, the invertebrate and water quality indices reached their worst point further below the paper mills. These indices (both oxygen-biased) hardly improved by the mouth, where the sewage fungus had much decreased. Different groups respond to different facets of pollution.

Sewage fungus was now well established upstream of the paper mills from the erstwhile minor pollutions. Downstream of the mills the amount was small—too small to show whether or not the mill pollution is contributing to its survival: a remarkable reversal which is, of course, due to the changes in the pollution itself.

When a river is grossly discoloured, and has sewage fungus reaching bloom status for over a kilometre, it is indeed polluted.

CHEMICAL IMPACTS

1. Peat (bog peat) influence

This traditionally affects the streams on and from the mountain bogs. In the early 1980s, the upper peat was being drained (drainage channels were cut deep, so erosion followed). Therefore more peat was, temporarily, entering the river. The water became browner and nutrient-poor species (e.g., *Callitriche hamulata, Myriophyllum alterniflorum*) became more frequent in the middle river.

2. **Channelling influence upstream**

This also was a 1980s phenomenon. In the mountain region, far too much of the typical streams was dredged (presumably also for drainage). The storm-swept gravel bars at the gentle edges of streams were replaced by steep, more stable slopes of disturbed (so more nutrient-rich) soil. Consequently fringe species such as *Juncus articulatus* and *Petasites hybridus* were replaced by fringing herbs such as *Mentha aquatica, Mimulus guttatus* agg. and *Myosotis scorpioides* (more nutrient-rich preference than their predecessors).

3. **Paper mill effluent**

There were two longstanding factories in the lower reaches. In 1969, their effluent was white, turbid and streaky. Sewage fungus was abundant, and the downstream community very poor ("e" on the Haslam & Wolseley index). With growing awareness of the damage done by river pollution, clean-up started, and by the mid-1980s there was no effect on the plants due to the lower mill and, by 1991, not even a short-lived effect from the effluent of the upper mill. Effluent from a nearby sewage treatment works also had no detectable effect. These, all still discharging effluent, show how possible it is (with money and goodwill) to improve effluents until they are apparently harmless. "Apparently", because (a) the lower river has other contaminants, so small effects could be masked, and (b) the amount of pollution which is acceptable in a large river may yet destroy the chemical environment of a small stream (1990).

GAINS

Improvements showed in the:

- increase of water-supported species by an average of two per 25m site between 1981 and 1987 (more, if starting from 1969 and 1978). Species included: *Ranunculus* spp., *Callitriche* spp., *Elodea canadensis, Potamogeton sparganifolius, Sparganium emersum*, and mosses.
- arrival of fringing herbs downstream of the effluents. Obviously fragments had been passing from upstream all the time, but established populations developed only with the clean-up (e.g., *Mentha aquatica, Mimulus guttatus* agg., *Myosotis scorpioides, Veronica beccabunga*). Polluted fringing herbs have poor root systems and are easily washed out, and slow to recover.
- increase of other short emergents, which are better-rooting and rather less sensitive to pollution than the fringing herbs (e.g., *Caltha palustris, Equisetum palustre*—Marsh horsetail, *Polygonum amphibium*).

- arrival of mosses downstream of the three effluents (factories, and sewage treatment works). Despite many bouldery reaches, which if clean would undoubtedly bear mosses, these were sparse or absent, except for the cleanest year of 1987.
- arrival of the nutrient-poor and pollution-sensitive *Callitriche hamulata* and *Myriophyllum alterniflorum*.
- complete loss of sewage fungus directly associated with the mills, which used to near-blanket the river.
- improvement of other effluents in the river, but their vegetation was studied less closely.

4. Improper use of herbicide

"Midstream" (a herbicide—probably diquat alginate) was mis-applied to the lower river in 1990, causing massive kills of vegetation including of the (probably best British population of the) rare *Potamogeton sparganifolius*. This was done for anglers: and should properly have been applied on the bed only, early in the year, to lessen future plant growth in salmon pools. (Not much blame attaches to anyone, as not enough was known about the effects at the time.) Fortunately, in 1991 the vegetation had much recovered.

In 1990, there was also over-use of herbicide on tall monocotyledon fringes. Such fringes, although sometimes annoying to anglers, protect banks from eroding in spate flows. It is expensive to mend banks! Spate flows wash away those fringes that extend into the river, away from the anchoring bank, and this "maintenance" comes free.

5. Increase of urbanisation with no corresponding increase in anti-pollution measures

On the outskirts of Aberdeen, and in nearby settlements, there was much development: housing, airport, supermarkets, industry. This was spread over a "large" area, the catchment of many small burns (streams). By 1990 the local river authority had noted 18 polluted incoming tributaries in this lower stretch, and these did not include the smallest, five of which were present and polluted by 1991 in the most-studied part. Sewage fungus and algae were again frequent, but not due to the factories. One was polluted for the first time in 1991. Those investigated were linked to development. Even a supermarket car park, when built above the river, had enough dirty run-off to be noticeable by its flourishing Blanket weed and lowered diversity in a swift, rocky (so well-oxygenated) part of the main river.

That is, the pollution effects are first noticed in the river plants, and exploration finds the (even only 0.5m wide) dirty tributary and follows it upstream to locate the source of the contamination.

Fig. 31

Glyceria maxima (Fig. 31) is one of the species whose shoots in the water become pale with (particularly organic) pollution (and usually on silt). In 1981, this yellowing occurred on the entry of tributaries polluted by both the airport and the factory effluents. From 1981 to 1985 the frequency of such yellowed sites decreased, but in 1986 it began to rise, being found in about half the recorded burns in 1989. Up to 1988, yellowed sites were at and downstream of the airport tributaries only. Thereafter they extended some miles upstream also.

6. Self-purification

The river cleans itself, transforms and removes many contaminants, from source to mouth. The pollutants needing cleaning are:

- agrochemicals from the farmed land covering most of the catchment (roughly stable);
- run-off from hard surfaces (getting worse rapidly);
- effluents from the occasional farm, industrial or house settlement, which have not yet been brought to modern standards;
- treated effluents (improving).

Throughout, the river plants and the stream both clean pollutants (primarily by microorganisms living on surfaces). Like a sewage treatment works, the Works can be overloaded, or receive contamination they cannot deal with. But they clean greatly, though less now so many minor streams are dried. The total area of such streams (area of purifying) is considerable.

7. Change of rock type

Most of the Don catchment is on resistant rock and, at the level of investigation reported here, its variations have no direct effect on the river vegetation (which is altered by topography, flow, downstream variation, and human impact).

However, in the upper catchment occasional outcrops of sandstone make vegetation changes visible at a glance. Where the sandstone starts, banks and hard substrate are immediately sandstone. A little further down unstable sediment and water become influenced by sandstone, and these continue to influence the plants for a short distance downstream of the return of resistant rock. So the upstream marking of sandstone is immediate, the downstream marking, a little fuzzy.

On the sandstone:

- the water-supported species (*Callitriche* spp., *Ranunculus* spp., etc.) increase in cover, e.g., from *c.* 15% to *c.* 80%. Both anchorage and nutrients are better for these species on the sandstone;
- the fringing herbs become more frequent, forming more of, or indeed fully, a fringe. Roots grow better, and can anchor better;
- because of the fringing herbs, cover and diversity (two of the standard measures) both increase. In short sandstone reaches there may be no new species but the increased frequency of each of the resistant rock species increases site diversity on the sandstone;
- because of the increase in fringing herbs (a generally mesotrophic group) the floral analyses show a skewing to mesotrophic, even when the sandstone is in an upstream generally moorland area.

Most sandstones are of higher nutrient status than resistant rocks, partly as the sandstone rock, partly as the nutrient-rich silt it gives rise to in the river bed. As usual, the vegetation change draws attention to itself and its potential causes, and observation—and the use of a geological map—show the cause is rock type.

NON-CHEMICAL CHANGES

1. Drought and high-flow summers

In drought summers the water level is lower on the banks, leaving more exposed "edge" ground, and additionally there are (probably) fewer storm flows. This allows:

- fringing herbs, small grasses and other short emergents to colonise more, and to grow more as there is more time between wash-outs (this is separable from the effects of pollution, because drought affects the whole river; pollution, only downstream of its entry);
- tall monocotyledon bands, if composed of suitable species, can grow out further into the river. *Sparganium erectum*, a river more than a bank species, can grow out particularly far in the river, though *Glyceria maxima* can come

out some way as being firmly anchored only to the bank. Sometimes this band extends 3m or more into the river channel. The next spate flow will find resistance from these clumps. Resistance increases because the plants cover more of the flow channel.Then spates will wash them away. Because of this added resistance, and the interlocking of the mosaic of rhizomes, more of the band is likely to be removed than if it was narrower. Therefore, in some places all the tall monocots are taken away, leaving bare areas which can be quickly colonised by fringing herbs—until the slower-growing tall monocotyledons arrive and shade them out;

- *Lemna minor* (Duckweed, Fig. 32), washed into the river, can grow well and form good populations in indentations in the bank and similar sheltered places—and get caught and grow in those dense water-supported plants reaching the water surface;
- silt is deposited on sides, shoals and islands which provide habitat and nutrients, especially for species upstream that cannot grow unless they have this extra resource.

In high-flow summers the reverse occurs. There is less habitat for fringing herbs, tall monocotyledon bands remain narrow, and there is little or no Lemna minor and silting. With this decrease in diversity, it is important to understand the habitat, and not attribute the loss to increased pollution!

Fig. 32

2. Drying: drainage and abstraction

As always, the farmers' wish for drier farmland means drainage and the drying of smaller streams. In the hilly middle reaches in the 1970s, streams formerly bearing only water-supported plants, instead bore more easily scoured emerged plants, such as *Mimulus guttatus* agg. (see Fig. 6b). These were previously restricted to the banks. By 1990, many more were dry and grassed over, or at any rate too dry for a good river plant community.

Abstraction is partly by factories, which return the water to the river some tens of metres downstream (and, in the most-studied part, do not take enough water to harm the main river). But abstraction is also for mains supplies, and this water is lost to the river. If, once depth and discharge are lowered, they still fall within the optimum range for the species (or improve them to the optimum) this will not damage the habitat.

Where the river becomes too shallow for the water-supported species which were there before, these decrease in frequency and cover, and so in site diversity also. At the same time the shallow-water habitat at the river edges becomes wider, and emergents can invade and colonise the new habitat (subject, of course, to spate flows). The characteristic way of recognising severely abstracted sites—and indeed sites equally severely affected by drought—is that compared with a reference site the diversity and cover of water-supported species is too low. If that of emergents is too high, that is supporting evidence for the diagnosis.

Other evidence is required (e.g., knowing the rainfall) to distinguish between sites dried by abstraction (which will be long-term, and the vegetation may, but often does not, adjust) or by drought (which is usually for 1–2 years only).

3. General habitats

As in all rivers, separate factors also make habitats suitable or less suitable for vegetation. The River Don ranges from mountain to lowland, from moor to urban, and there are, for example, mills on tributaries, places where livestock drink—all the ordinary hindrances to good vegetation. In the lower river there are, as usual, parts too deep (or unstable) for macrophytes, and vegetation at the shallow sides has to be used for interpretation. There are shaded reaches, where vegetation is reduced or even removed through lack of light. There are bridges, with piers and lined banks, which shade and alter substrates both directly and indirectly (either by piers or by a small weir associated with the bridge) causing alterations in flow, depth and substrate around the bridge: and so alterations in vegetation. There are constructed channels, there are weirs. All alter habitat, and so, potentially, vegetation.

THE YEAR 1987

The year of 1987 had the highest quality of vegetation in the lower river in the years between 1969 and 1991. By 1987, the effluents entering the river were reasonably clean. And although the number of polluted tributaries was increasing, their effects were not yet serious.

In 1988, vegetation quality was down, which was puzzling. Effluents, weather, disturbance, herbicide: none of these accounted for the deterioration.

Just one of those things? No: by 1989 the reason was clear: more pollution in the streams of the airport area. It is very sad when so much trouble has been put into a clean-up and new pollutions arrive to undo most of the good of this clean-up. The calculated damage ratings downstream of the factories and sewage treatment effluents were similar in the early 1980s and early 1990s.

And the River Don is no more complex than other rivers of its size! Its complexities may be different, habitat variations are many, but to interpret whole rivers, aquatic plant behaviour must be understood (see Tables 2 and 3 at the end of this book).

> ...And note, I am sure I missed a lot. Ecology is not simple! (S.M. Haslam)

STAYING STABLE

Examples are few, and the best studied are not English, nor British...but German! There are surely British examples in unpopulous places like Assynt in Scotland, but in lowland (mainly) Bavaria, in good agricultural country, there are stable streams. These paint quite a different picture to that described above. However, British records *c.* 1968–1980, although over but a short time, paint the same picture.

Why? An important factor is that water level and flow stayed satisfactory. Germany, like most European countries, drained its land much less than did Britain, before 1950, so the streams had an initial advantage. The maintenance engineering on the streams was "normal" with no long-term disruption. Chemical status varied only little; and the vegetation also varied only little.

CONCLUSION

Well! Just water weeds, unchanging and of little interest? Hardly! More of a demonstration, for students and naturalists alike, of changes, and the sensitivity of river communities to their environment, and indeed of the speed of their response. Do you have a stream near you? With plants in? Why not look and plot this summer, and try again next year and the next, and see what changes. And look at why it has changed, too.

TABLES

Table 1. Vegetation losses mainly *c.* 1980–2010. River Lark (Temple Bridge), Icklingham, Suffolk. Except for *Potamogetons* (which were lost by the 1970s), the main loss is after 1980, and is dramatic. The slow, and indeed the fast shallow habitats, have been lost with engineering (engineers like uniformity).

(Faster Flow)	*1930s*	*1950s*	*1970s*	*1990s*	*2000s*
Ranunculus fluitans	d	d	ld		
Oenanthe fluviatilis	f		f		
Groenlandia densa	f	d ALONG MUCH	o		
Sparganium emersum	r		o		
Apium nodiflorum	r		l		
Berula erecta	r		-		
Moss	r		l		
(Moderate Flow)					
*Sparganium emersum**	d		f		d
Sagittaria sagittifolia	sd		o+		
Potamogeton perfoliatus	f		o+		
Elodea canadensis	f	NO FURTHER RECORD	o+		
Potamogeton crispus	f		lf		
Callitriche sp.	o		o	l	l
Potamogeton praelongus	r		-		
Potamogeton pusillus	r		-		
(Slow Flow)					
Potamogeton lucens	d		-		
Potamogeton pectinatus	sd		-	d	
Potamogeton natans	f		-		
Nuphar lutea	f		-		
Sparganium emersum	f	NO SLOW HABITAT			
Sparganium erectum	o		o	o	o
Zannichellia palustris	o		l		
Scirpus lacustris	r		o		

Frequency codes: d—dominant; sd—sub-dominant; a—abundant; f—frequent; o—occasional; s—sparse; l—local; r—rare.

* *Sparganium emersum*, no slow-flow habitat in the 2000s.

Table 2. Macrophyte improvement in the Lower Don, Scotland.

a) Damage rating	1969	1978	1981	1983	1984	1986	1987
Upstream of paper mills, Hatton			a	a	a	a	a
Parkhill	b	b	b	a	a	a	a
Downstream of both mills. Persley Bridge	e	d	c	b	b	b	b
Grandhome Bridge			c	a	a/b	a/b	a
Seaton			b	a	b	a	b

b) Average site diversity *(No. of upstream sites 11; downstream sites 12, not all surveyed each year)*	1981	1983	1984	1986	1987
Upstream of mills	9	10	10	9	10
Between mills	5	6	7	8	10
Downstream of mills	7	7	8	9	10

c) No. of sites with fringing herbs *(Short bushy emergents, Mimulus, Myosotis, Veronica, etc.)*	1981	1983	1984	1986	1987
Upstream of mills	15	12	10	7	7
Between mills	0	1	0	16	8
Downstream of mills	0	2	5	14	11

d) No. of sites with Mosses *(Prominent, all species)*	1981	1983	1984	1986	1987
Upstream of mills	6	6	6	5	6
Between mills	3	4	6	3	9
Downstream of mills	2	4	1	0	3

Table 3. Plant deterioration in the Lower Don, Scotland.

a) No. of sites with yellowed *Glyceria maxima* *(in water, on mud)*	1981	1983	1984	1986	1987	1988
Upstream of mills	4	3	1	3	2	5
Between mills	1	1	1	1	3	4
Downstream of mills	4	0	1	0	5	6

b) No. of sites with sewage fungus	1981	1983	1984	1986	1987	1988
Upstream of mills	0	0	0	1	1	5
Between mills	1	2	3	4	0	5
Downstream of mills	6	4	5	5	0	3
	(2 much)	(1 much)	(3 much)			

(Sewage fungus varies greatly with temperature and flow. Note the upstream gain and downstream increase.)

THE RIVER FRIEND SERIES

This series of small books is designed for people with a general or specific interest in rivers.

Please visit the River Friend Website for an up to-date list of

PUBLISHED Titles: **https://www.riverfriend.tinasfineart.uk**

Standalone* Titles in the Series include:

A PROLOGUE TO THE SERIES: Plant identification and Glossary of Terms (ISBN 978 1 9162096 2 6)

DRYING UP (ISBN 978 1 9162096 1 9)

STREAM STORY I: A Riveting Riverscape—River Brue, Somerset (ISBN 978 1 9162096 0 2)

INTERPRET: What do Plants Tell us? (ISBN 978 1 9162096 5 7)

REED—ON THE EDGE (ISBN 978 1 9162096 4 0)

An Introduction to the WATER FRAMEWORK DIRECTIVE (ISBN 978 1 9162096 3 3)

WATER: Clean and Dirty (ISBN 978 1 9162096 7 1)

***VEGETATION CHANGES OVER TIME Is there freeze frame?* (ISBN 978 1 9162096 6 4)**

STREAM STORY: Another Riveting Riverscape—River Cam, Cambridge

AWFUL ALIENS: Foreign Plants of the River and its Banks

WHAT RIVERS DO FOR US

LOOK AT THE BOTTOM

STREAM STORY: A Brook in Transit: Bourn Brook, Cambridge

* Each book is about a different subject so the series can be read in any order

ABOUT THE AUTHORS

Sylvia Haslam is a botanist and river culture, etc., specialist. Anyone wanting to find out more should look at the publications list on her website (**https://www.riversandreeds.co.uk**). Her publications specific to this series are listed in the book entitled *A PROLOGUE TO THE SERIES: Plant identification and Glossary of Terms*.

Tina Bone has worked as a self-employed Desktop Publisher for many years until she changed career to work as a Professional Artist and Book Publisher from March 2005. To view Tina's résumé and artwork please visit her website: **https://www.tinasfineart.uk**.

www.ingramcontent.com/pod-product-compliance
Ingram Content Group UK Ltd.
Pitfield, Milton Keynes, MK11 3LW, UK
UKHW062255290726
14090UKWH00017B/700

9 781916 209664